FOREX

CANDLESTICK SIMPLIFIELD

REMOVING THE NOISE FROM THE CHART

HOW TO MAKE CONSISTENT PROFIT TRADING JUST THREE CATEGORIES OF CANDLESTICK PATTERN

Abraham Robert. C

In order to say thank you for purchasing this book, I offer the below video course and more to you as a token of appreciation

__Find the Link to the bonus video courses at the end of this book__

TABLE OF CONTENT

Chapter 1

A BREIF SUMMARY ON

CANDLESTICK

Because they are more visually appealing, candlestick charts are the most often used charts among forex traders. Compared to other charts, such as a bar or line chart, candlestick charts more clearly show the open and close of various time periods.

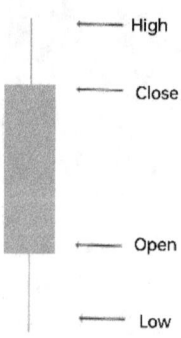

Traders analyze price patterns and candlestick formations to determine when to enter and quit the market. Individual forex candlesticks may create a variety of candle forms, including the shooting star, hammer, and hanging man.

Additionally, several price patterns such as wedges, triangles, and head-and-shoulders patterns are formed on forex candlestick charts.

These candle formations and patterns are common on forex charts, but they also apply to other markets, such as stocks and cryptocurrencies.

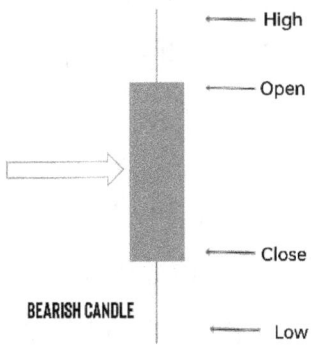

A candlestick is made up of three distinct points: the open, the close, and the wicks. If the closing price is higher than the open, the candle will become green or blue—the exact colour depends on the chart settings. If the closing price is less than the open, the candle will become red.

When the chart is set to a daily view, each candle signifies a single day, with the open price signifying the first trade of the day and the close price signifying the final deal of the day.

Open price: When a new candle is forming, the open price shows the first trading price.

The upper wick's top is expensive. The high price is the closing price of a bullish candle or the open price of a bearish candle if there is no upper wick.

The lower wick's bottom is the low price. The low price is either the closing price of a bearish candle or the open price of a bullish candle if there isn't a lower wick.

Close price: The last price exchanged during the candle's creation is known as the close price.

A technical tool for forex research, a candlestick chart shows price activity by displaying individual candles on a chart.

Forex traders who use candlestick price action must be able to determine the opening and closing prices as well as the highs and lows of the market for a certain time frame.

An understanding of trends and reversals may be gained by traders via the application of price action analysis.

For instance, clusters of candlesticks may create patterns on forex charts and diagrams that can suggest trend reversals or continuations. Additionally, candlesticks may develop unique shapes that might signal market entry for buy or sell.

The Body

The price range between the opening and closing prices over a certain period of time is represented by the candlestick bodies. A body that is black or crimson often indicates that the price closed higher than it opened.

Stated differently, the price began at a low point, increased during the course of the transaction, and ended at a higher point. We refer to this candlestick as a bullish candlestick.

A white or green body, on the other hand, indicates that the price closed lower than it opened. We refer to this candlestick as a bearish candlestick. However, the colors are subject to change according on the charting platform you choose.

The wick or shadow

The thin lines on top and bottom of a candlestick's body are the candlestick shadows, often referred to as wicks or tails. There are crucial hints about the trading session provided by these upper and lower shadows. The highest price of the session is shown by an upper shadow, while the lowest price is indicated by a lower shadow.

Additionally, traders may change the hues of their candlesticks on their trading platform since everything looks better in color.

Since color television is superior than black and white television, it would make sense to add some color to the candlestick charts as well. Traders just need to use a red candle in place of a white one, and a green candle in place of a black one.

This indicates that the candlestick would be green if the closing price exceeded the beginning price.

On the other hand, the candlestick would be red if the price ended lower than it started.

The future price direction of the currency pairings may be accurately predicted by the candlestick patterns. Candlestick patterns may be used in conjunction with other technical indicators to bring you verified market indications that are far less likely to be misleading.

Three Essential Candlestick Chart Elements

- The whole candle's size and length
- Relationship between the close and open
- Shadows and their relationship to the candle's body

The whole candle's size and length

It is not uncommon to have candles that open at the low, shut at the high, or are very lengthy. Such a candle signals a significant trend reversal is happening if there has been a prolonged downturn. Conversely, after a protracted upswing, we are talking about fatigue if an exceptionally long candle closes, which would indicate a lengthy wick to the upside or a powerful bearish body straight from the top.

Relationship Between the Close and Open

When the market is bullish or experiencing a significant rally, purchasing will often happen at the open. A white, hollow candle should develop as the price rises. The length, or difference, between the open and the close, indicates the bulls' dominance over the market's price activity.

A dark body candle should appear in a bad market or during a significant slump. This is a representation of sellers dominating that specific moment when they join the market on the open. Unlike bar charts, candlestick charts provide excellent analysis of the body color and form of the candle.

Shadows and Their Relation to the Candle's Body

When compared to the open and close prices shown in the actual candle body, the length of the wick indicates the price low and/or high. It may also demonstrate the market's rejection of a support or resistance level. If lengthy tails, or shadows, are seen at the base of the body, it is crucial to determine whether or not these formations follow a protracted downward trend. This suggests that the trend may eventually run its course and that either supply is growing or demand is decreasing.

Particularly after a protracted price increase, the formation of tails, or shadows, at the tops of real bodies suggests that supply is rising and demand is contracting. It is more crucial to examine the shadow in respect to the actual body the bigger it is, since this might indicate how strong the reversal is.

Strong Momentum Candles

Marubozu candles are strong momentum candles that often open at a resistance or support level. A momentum candle with a little tail or none at all is called a Marubozu candle. When it comes to price movement, this particular kind of candlestick pattern is quite significant and potent. Strong purchasing off support or strong selling off resistance are terms used by Marubozu. In Japanese, marubozu means "bald head" or "shaved head."

This is due to the fact that a candle of this kind either has no shadow at all or a very little shadow. In contemporary market trading, a Marubozu may still be regarded as legitimate even if it has extremely little wicks on both sides. The phrase "momentum candle" is used for this reason.

In an upward trend, a white Marubozu candle may indicate a continuance; conversely, in a downward trend, it may indicate a possible bullish reversal pattern.

The future price direction of the currency pairings may be accurately predicted by the candlestick patterns. Candlestick patterns may be used in conjunction with other technical indicators to bring you verified market indications that are far less likely to be misleading.

The dependability of a candlestick pattern is affected by the following three factors:

Trade environment

The dependability of a candlestick pattern rises if it appears in a trading environment with close support (where falling prices stop falling and start rising) and resistance (where rising prices stop rising and start dropping) levels.

Time frame

Longer timeframes: Because markets are less volatile throughout these periods, candlestick patterns provide trustworthy market indications. Extended periods enable patterns to function in varying market circumstances to determine a certain outcome instead of making snap judgements that result in erroneous signals.

Size of pattern

Because larger candlestick patterns take into account notable price fluctuations in the market and provide traders powerful market signals, they produce more dependable outcomes. The trustworthiness of a pattern increases with the number of candlesticks in it and vice versa.

Chapter 2

CANDLESTICK WITH BODY

The first on my list of three candles is candlestick with body.

When compared to other candlestick patterns on the chart, the Big Body Candlestick is a single-bar pattern with a huge true body. The body of the candlestick, or the difference between the starting and closing prices, is much bigger than the usual candlesticks that surround it.

Strong investor sentiment is indicated by the period of significant purchasing or selling activity.

Bullish Big Body Candlestick: The price at which it closes is much higher than its opening. This is usually seen as a positive indication since it shows significant purchasing pressure.

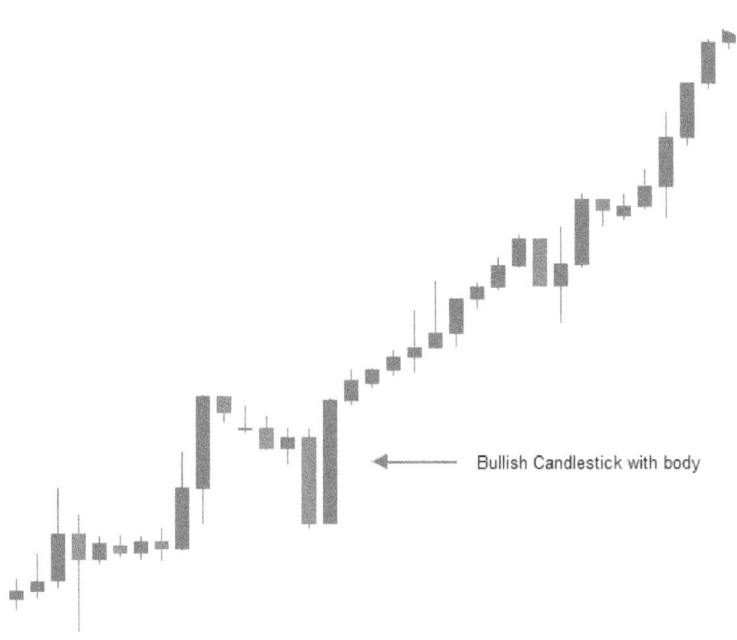

Bullish Candlestick with body

Bearish Big Body Candlestick: This kind of candlestick is usually seen as bearish since the open price is much higher than the closing price, indicating strong selling pressure.

The huge body candlestick is a flexible pattern for both short-term and long-term traders since it may show up on charts with any period, from minutes to months.

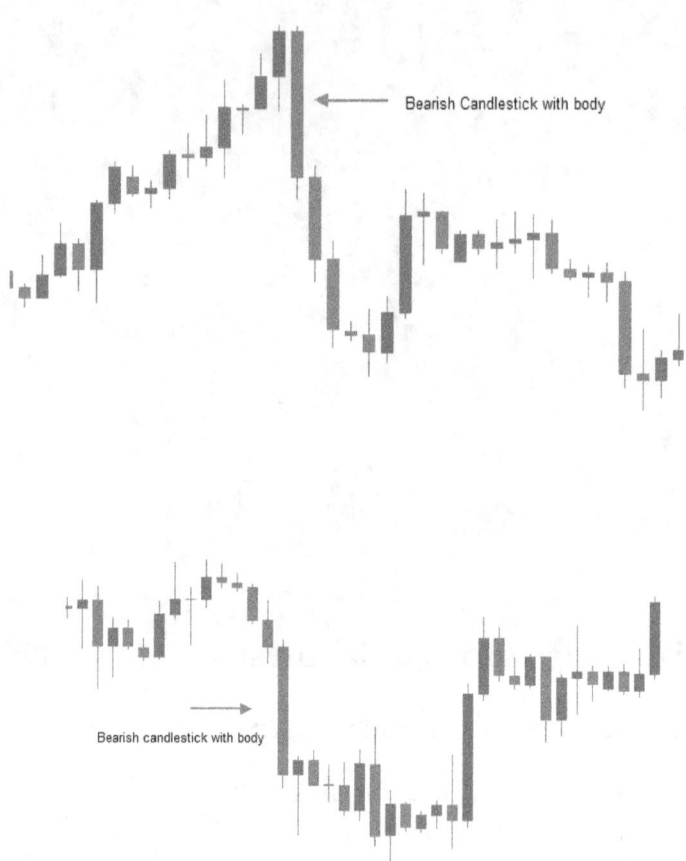

Identifying Big Body Candlesticks

A few essential traits to look for while identifying a Big Body Candlestick are as follows:

- The candlestick's body is notably bigger than the ones around it.
- There might be little or no wicks on the candlestick. But the pattern remains valid even with wicks present.
- In order to validate the strong emotion, the volume throughout the period should preferably be greater than the average.

How to Trade Candlesticks

Big-body candlestick traders must be aware of the possible change in momentum that they may indicate. Here are some rules to follow:

Confirm with Volume: A large body candlestick with high volume indicates a strong confidence in the direction of the price movement, making it more meaningful.

Wait for more confirmation: To verify the pattern, wait for a few intervals or the following candle. If you're looking for a bullish huge body, keep moving upward. On a bearish large body, keep an eye out for more declines.

Examine the General Trend: Large body candlesticks may signify a possible reversal in the trend or its continuance. Once again, determining the pattern's importance requires a grasp of the larger market environment.

Crucial Advice for Trading big-Body Candlesticks

Understand the Market Context: Large body candlesticks cannot be read in a vacuum. They belong in the larger context of the market and trend. It is essential to comprehend the prevailing trend, levels of support and resistance, and psychological pricing points.

Use Confirming Indicators: To validate the indications provided by large body candlesticks, use other technical analysis tools. Further information on the momentum and volatility behind the price move may be obtained by using indicators such as the Bollinger Bands, Moving Average Convergence Divergence (MACD), and Relative Strength Index (RSI).

Wait for confirmation: Refrain from jumping into a trade the moment you see a large body candlestick. To validate the indication, watch for more price movement in the next periods.

This might manifest as a separate pattern that validates the first signal, or it could take the shape of another massive body candlestick.

Manage Your Risk: It's critical to put effective risk management techniques into practice. Establish stop-loss levels, stick to your risk tolerance, and only invest money you can afford to lose.

Chapter 3

CANDLESTICK WITH WICK

REJECTION

The second on my list of three candles is candlestick with wick rejection or candlestick with shadow

The peak and low points of the price movement within a certain time frame are shown by the candle's wick length. Important tradeable chances might be presented to forex traders by comprehending and using candlestick wicks.

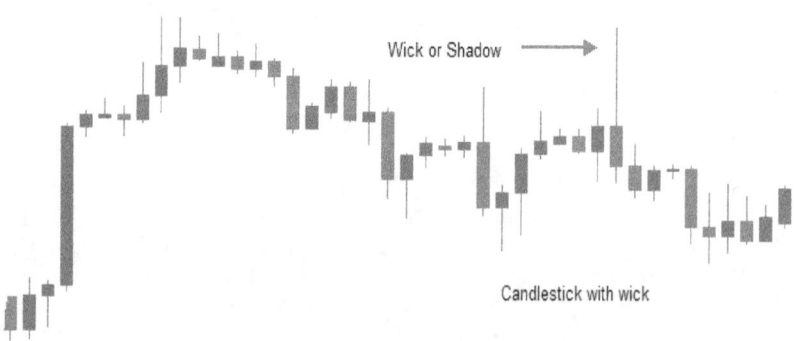

A gravestone like shooting stars with a long wick candle Dojis and hammers belong to a "family" of reversal candlesticks, but depending on the direction of the market and the location at which the candle is forming, this candle may also often be a continuation candle.

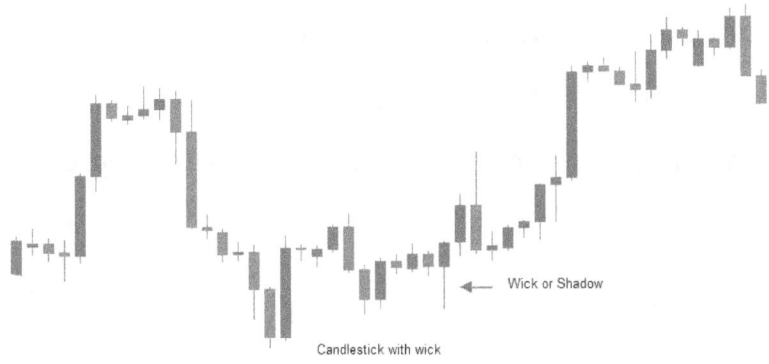

Candlestick with wick

Beginners may not realize this, but one of the most crucial elements of candlestick charts is the wick, or shadow. This is so because the candle's trading range is represented by the wick, which is a thin line that extends from the top or bottom of the candle. Candlestick wick analysis is the technique of analyzing these wicks to identify potential trading opportunities.

Types of wicks

Candlesticks may have upper and lower wicks; the upper wick is located above the body of the candlestick, while the lower wick is the one that protrudes from the base. The top wick of the candle represents the price that was the most it has ever been, and the lower wick represents the lowest.

An upper and lower wick, as well as a short or long wick, may be included on a candle, which shows the range of prices between the highest and lowest point during the given time period.

Long Wicks

A lengthy upper wick indicates that after buyers pushed the price up initially, sellers took control and the price went down again. However, a long lower wick sticking out of the bottom indicates that, despite sellers driving the price down at initially, buyers eventually took back control and the price rose.

A lengthy wick suggests that there could be strong support or resistance at that level. Indecisiveness in the market is indicated if the candle body is tiny and the wicks are about equal in length on both sides.

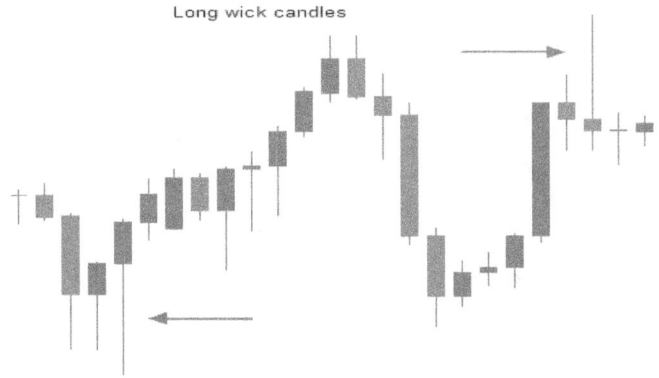

Long wick candles

Short Wicks

A short wick is one that is much shorter or smaller than the body of the candle. It indicates that there wasn't much price rejection at that point.

A rising candle with a short top wick suggests that buyers were in control and that there wasn't much selling pressure at that point.

Conversely, a lowering or negative candle with a short bottom wick indicates that the sellers are in control. A short wick indicates that there is weak resistance or support at that level.

Short wick candles

Candlestick wick research is essential for traders since it provides insight into the market's sentiment. The wick, which represents the price range across the time period, may be used to gauge the strength of buying or selling pressure at a certain price point. A long wick denotes strong resistance or support at that level as opposed to a short wick, which denotes weak support or resistance. Understanding the effects of various wick kinds is crucial for traders to make informed trading choices.

How to trade a candle with a wick

Finding a trend is the first step.

If you see one or more candles in a downtrend that have longer wicks at the top, it indicates that there is a good chance the price will fall down in the direction of the market.

When a long wick appears at the bottom or peak of a short trend, it may be traded as a reversal pattern.

Resistance or support levels must attest to it or validate it. Support is the point at which a respite in the downward trend is possible. The opposite of a support level is resistance.

A long wick candle often appears when a trend is coming to an end and the price action reversals right away to create a new, opposing trend.

Wicks are useful for determining important levels such as resistances and supports. With this knowledge, traders might initiate a long position and set a stop loss below the support level. Finding possible reversal points may also be aided by identifying strong supports or resistance points.

Whereas a short wick implies weak support or resistance, a long wick indicates strong support or resistance at that level.

If you're in an uptrend, a lengthy upper wick may signal that buyers are losing steam and sellers are starting to take the initiative. If you are in a downtrend, a lengthy lower wick may indicate that buyers are beginning to join the market and that the trend may be losing steam.

Candlestick Wick Analysis's advantages

The following are a few benefits of candlestick wick analysis:

Shows price changes visually

A clear and succinct depiction of the price's changes may be seen in candlestick charts.

The wicks show the range of prices in which the item moved, while the candlestick body shows the beginning and closing values. This enables traders to identify patterns and trends in the market with ease and speed.

Determines important price point

Candlestick wick analysis is a useful tool for traders to identify critical price levels, such as reversal points or levels of support and resistance. By looking at the length and placement of the wicks, traders may identify these pivotal price points and choose the greatest trading chances.

Reflects market sentiments

Candlestick wick research may provide valuable insights into market mood. By analyzing these patterns, traders may get a deeper understanding of market mood and make more informed trading choices.

Helps confirm trends

Candlestick wick analysis may also be used to validate trends; when combined with other technical indicators, it becomes even more reliable and useful for trading decision-making.

Chapter 4

INDECISION CANDLE

The third on my list of three candles is indecision candlesticks

When traders see the indecisive candlestick pattern at a support or resistance level, they often get confused.

Unknown to many, the indecision candlestick is a rather powerful indicator that may complement any forex trader's price movement technical trading tactics flawlessly.

The indecision candle is often connected with terms like Doji or the Spinning Top. The nature and construction of the Doji and the Spinning Top are comparable.

Although indecisive candlesticks are unable to provide traders with any clues about the direction the market may go in the future, they might still be useful to forex traders on occasion.

These patterns often appear on market charts when there is strong buying and selling pressure that is maintained at a rapid speed.

A pattern's body must be relatively tiny and centered within the candle range in order for it to even be considered a candle. Typically, that place falls in between the highs and the lows.

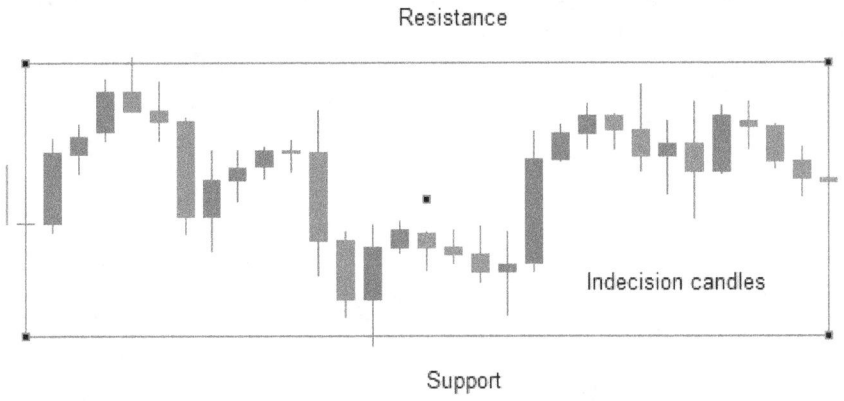

In addition, the wicks of the indecision candle need to be quite long and visible on both sides of the body. The lengths of these wicks are also proportional.

These proportional wicks are said to be a sign that, throughout a typical trading cycle, the price has tried to go both upward and downward.

These swings in price direction basically indicate that the market was unable to sustain either high or low levels during that specific trading session.

This indicates that there was intense competition between the bulls and bears throughout the alleged trading session.

A group of Indecsion candles

It's also worth noting that the market will essentially close in the same vicinity as it began during the first session after an incident of this magnitude.

Because neither the bulls nor the bears were able to secure a definitive victory, this is a clear indication of indecisiveness in the market and is why the candlestick is named "indecisive."

Making The Most of Indecisive Candlesticks

If you want them to be, these candlesticks—especially those that appear in strategic locations on a trader's chart—can be very effective price reversal indicators.

The trader may begin preparing for a potential trend reversal or, if the market conditions are favorable, even forecasting the end of a countertrend retracement after he has effectively determined their importance.

Additionally, the market's back-and-forth fight between bullish and bearish forces generates a spike in volatility that presents a few chances for traders who can spot the gaps in time.

CONLUSION

Note: focusing mainly on these three categories of candles help to remove the noise from the chart, no matter what the market is doing, stick and wait for this category of candles to play out and don't just enter a trade because there played out, you should wait for other confirmation, and try to identify if they are playing out on a major support or resistance area.

There are numerous candlesticks in the market, but you don't actually need all to be a successful trader. The forex industry is very wide, for you to be consistently profitable you need to learn to be specific in your approach, stick to something simple that work and stay on it consistently.

In the long run you will see yourself being profitable as you keep repeating the same setup over and over again.

GET INSTANT ACCESS TO THE FREE VIDEO COURSE BY FOLLOWING THE BELOW LINK

subscribepage.io/freeforexcourse

Click or copy and paste the above link on your browser for instant access to the bonus video.

Happy Trading!

www.ingramcontent.com/pod-product-compliance
Lightning Source LLC
Chambersburg PA
CBHW062304290526
45794CB00006B/2691